-

Release You

-

Ash Coulson

I shouldn't have to regret getting help,

Trying to get better,

Hoping for healing,

When now I know,

Clear as nighttime,

I will always hurt like this.

Half of my life

I've been

Scared of

You

Me

Everyone

Do not call me 'Dad,'

From now

Until forever

No words truer have been spoken than

The only way to avoid disappointment, is to

never

Expect;

Anticipate;

Want;

Love.

I wish it wasn't this way.

Cutting is like bad sex;

It's never worth it.

Guilty

Guilty

Guilty

Guilty

Guilty

Guilty

Guilty

Guilty

Guilty

Guilty

Guilty

Guilty

Guilty

Guilty

Guilty

Guilty

Guilty

Guilty

There is no one less deserving of your desire,

So why me?

Lying to all those I love

Is easy for me.

This troubles me some.

Fuck,

Drink,

Smoke,

Go back to sleep.

God is a real cunt.

There is no one else with the power to lessen the suffering of their creations, the ones that, supposedly, they love unconditionally.

Yet,

Here we are,

Pain, turmoil alike.

Maybe we already are in hell.

Everyone* likes dick,

But

Not everyone likes men.

Love is a feeling

Most apparent

When he is on his knees.

Crack,

Crack,

Crack,

Crack,

Crack,

Crack,

Crack,

Crack,

Crack,

Crack.

I want to break all my fucking fingers.

I still think of you

When I'm all alone

I still remember you

When everyone sleeps

I still miss you

When I run out of distractions.

I say

I'm fine

But very often,

I really am not.

I do not like

Them

Putting chemicals in the water

That

Turn the frickin

Frogs gay.

Once

There was a melody

Once

There was a song

Once

I belonged

Once

There was symmetry

Once

I thought I was free.

It's almost better

Not to know

Of all the things they do and feel in my

absence.

I hope that you had fun

I hope you're okay now, and are doing alright

I still care about you, but

I don't want to see you anymore.

I know you had stuff going on

I know that maybe you needed me

You loved me most when I laid back, and

opened my mouth

I didn't like how it bruised and hurt for weeks

Hiding from everyone, my aching cheeks

While I appreciate the things you bought

I am not that strong

I am left here

Not knowing how to love

Not knowing where my head is

Where I want to go

It should be my choice to decide if I should do

it

Not yours

It's my life, my blood

Not yours

Part of me hopes that you read this

My tyrannical prince,

My dangerously handsome,

Regrettably sexy,

Meltingly hot,

Temptingly wealthy,

Possessing alcohol, cigarettes, and everything

in-between,

Unrelentingly suave when horny,

Apologetic after the fact,

My sweet tasting

Prince.

What happens next, I have no idea. Sensuality, sexuality, and romanticism shall be the end of me, my dear. I wish to desire, and to be desired. I wish to discard my pride, and lay myself bare, both in mind and in body, to someone equally devoid of pride. I have no restful nights; I only lie awake, and I dream nightmares of being alone, being unloved, unwanted. If even I do not love, nor want myself, then there should be no possibility of anyone else doing so. Who I want looks like soft lighting and midnight sheets, they house intrigue beneath the covers. They smell of cheap vodka, smoke, and sweat. The feeling they evoke is akin to Damnation and Salvation sharing the same space; chaotic; beautiful; ecstatic. All that is heard of them in our space is their intoxicated moans, satisfied sighs, and ragged breaths. They taste like cheap wine, cigarettes, and like longing. Mon cherie, thy name is Desire, and how I wish to be completely yours. Goodnight, and sanguinely, not goodbye.

wistful longing,

ash.

Black cat,

White cat,

All cats,

Good cats.

Your affection was a painful little monster, but it has touched me in ways the stars could not.

Fatherhood must be

The world's most difficult thing to do

Judging by its rate of failure

And by the number of lonely children that are

left to feel unworthy and unloved.

Everything important to you will be thrown
out of the door
Just like a Frisbee.

Being a faggot

Doesn't make me special

For any reason.

Red

Orange

Green

Blue

These are the colours that remind me of you

Shining Lights around my bedroom

Feelings swept under with a broom

Christmas Star on the tree

Crossing Scars on my wrists

I will grow older

Waiting for you as it gets colder

If I could change your mind

Go back in time

Make you believe again

If I go could go back in time

Make you see again

Stars fell from her lips

Ghosts trapped behind her eyes

Wrists bound above her head

 Blinded by cloth

On her face

A smile

With narrow eyes

I held her knees

Pink flowers etched in my arms

Stinging ribbons she carved in my back

Do it

She begged

Do it

She was manic

Please

She wanted nothing more

So

I relented;

Closed my eyes;

Thought of someone else;

Stars fell from her eyes.

You see me for who I am

But

With 10,000 layers

Of You.

I'd like to take a small tin boat

And float

All the way to the middle of the lake

All the way

Far enough that no one can see me

It'd be so cold

Cold enough to make my lips purple

Dark

Only broken by the orange of a cigarette

Tie

Bags of pebbles to my ankles

Dive

And melt away into the cold.

Sweet and Handsome,

Pokémon,

Kind and Emotional,

Basketball,

Strong in two ways,

Wooden Swords,

Reliable and Confused,

Fourth Grade,

Talkative to a fault,

Girls,

Hardworking,

Guitar.

Thank you for everything,

My dear, dear friend.

In the bed we used to share,

Wherein we looked a picturesque pair,

I've done reprehensible things,

My cross to bear.

In the bed you looked so beautiful in,

I've committed acts of sin.

You will never know what it is I did.

The guilt and knowledge wrap my head.

They force my mouth closed,

And leave the thoughts to rot and decay

without end.

In the bed that we used to share old memories,

I made new ones.

Evil ones, bad ones, horrible ones, they

scream and shout.

I want to gouge out my eyes, so they may all

fall out.

Too many beetles

They swim through my veins when I'm not

looking

They know when I try to see them, and they

stop moving

It doesn't hurt, it just bulges, and I imagine it

looks weird to anyone watching me

If there is something I need,

It is to remove my veins, thus taking the

beetles with them.

Hopefully they don't retreat into my heart.

Maybe

It's your dark, curled hair

Or even

Your closed eye smiles.

Maybe

It's the way you hold me when I can't stop

from crying, how you care

Or

The way you make everything stop swirling,

even if just for a while.

It could be

Your lips, that lead me to nirvana

I wonder if

The sensation that is your skin against mine

Is what has me addicted to you?

Like what heroin used to be,

Or even a newer vice I've found in 40oz. of

caramel licorice.

Every time I look into your eyes

I see it.

Every time I hear you sing

I hear it.

Who would have thought that this would

happen now?

The way you laugh

And how you look underneath me.

This feels like autumn

I don't know why I feel so much here.

It doesn't really matter, so long as there is a

Tomorrow with you.

I want to

Cut myself

In half

'I love you,'

Doesn't seem to mean much

To you at least.

My feelings are

As fickle

As possibility

I want to break my bones with sticks and
stones
And words are candle flame.

I've been sick

For far too long

And it, much too often,

Keeps me away from you.

I wonder if you could love me,

Just the way I am,

Sickness and everything.

The problem I have is this:

So long as you exist, the rest of the world

loses its charm.

Please, I implore you, my dear,

Consider this lonely and sad boy

As more than just a friend.

You're not the person I loved.

You're just a person that I used to know.

You break my heart

And as you do

I find myself still loving you.

I am stuck

I can't make you fall in love with me just the way I want you to.

My imagination made you perfect

Made you beautiful

Made me love you like I did

My imagination convinces me that there are

bugs in my skin, and explosives in the walls

My imagination told me to stick around

That you were worth it

My heart knows this not to be true

My thoughts are not to be trusted.

He was deeply flawed

Infinitely imperfect

Wounded

But still I kiss and cuddle him,

That broken, beautiful boy.

I wish you were better

I was so proud of you

You were doing so well

What happened?

Curse out all the things that make you feel like

a failure

Even with your impurities

You are important

To me at least.

You hold my hand

And look passionately into my eyes

You sip a coffee

And smile

And laugh

And look just so very lovely

The world grows a little warmer.

How many smokes does it take to get to my center?

Why do I always write about love?

Why do I always write about you?

Where has my time gone?

Where did the person I wanted to be leave to?

Do you remember where I first kissed you?

 Where I told you I had feelings for you?

How come I think you're so wonderful?

How can I be good enough?

Who is it that I am not?

Who should I have been?

What the fuck happened to me?

What do I do to get what I want, or seemingly, need?

I know you don't have the answers.

I should give up, just like I do with all things.

I am stupid for hoping.

Snoring;

Warm body;

Cold feet;

Soft breath;

Lips;

Alone in your company;

Endless;

Light kisses:

Tiny smile;

Desire;

Remiss;

Sleepless;

Eventually;

Maybe;

Maybe not;

Probably not;

Motivation;

Discouragement;

Hope;

Disappointment;

Please make it stop.

The pink ribbons you leave

Trap me in the

Ecstasy of perversion

Fuck me until I think of nothing else.

He cites my birth as a

Consequence

Of tight, sweet, pussy.

Sexism is a fatherly trait.

I have nothing left besides this

Since I have been sober.

Give me all I want from you

To replace fumes long yearned.

O mommy dearest,

When did I become so

Reprehensible?

Beautiful Lady.

Very Liked.

Maybe even loved.

The most painful death

Is the one

That never comes.

Just because bad things have happened to me

Doesn't mean that

I'm deserving of your love.

You're why I love the mornings.

The rising sun is your smile;

The smell of the rain is the feeling of your
hands on mine;

The tea I drink in the morning is the tea I
share with you.

When you adjust yourself against me,

It's the comforting warmth of a smoke.

I never want to leave you, just like my bed.

The music I hear is the music that we dance
to.

Your kisses are like my dreams.

I wish nobody loved me.

I could leave without protest.

Without fear of making anyone sad.

Satisfy your carnal hunger

With my flesh

I am no more than a means to an end.

I don't forget you

When I love others

With all the passion I give to you

I still think of you when I lie awake, and when

I dream soft dreams.

My love is not finite

Even if she breaks my heart

I would be remiss

Not to love her completely

Get rid of sad feelings

Via tears

Her voice is the blooming of lilacs

What happened to us?

You look so nice today.

Did you put highlights in your hair?

Did you get new glasses?

How's your family?

I guess I'll never know.

I will forever have love for you.

Thanks for the things we shared.

Lips, curls, freckles.

I ripped and tore my flesh

Blood seeps into your clothes

I can't stop

You look at me with horror

I wish you would let me die

When it gets late like this

All I want is to

Hold you, in my arms,

And a cigarette, in my lips.

There's nothing quite like

Becoming the parent

You've loathed your entire life

Happiness*

C'est ce

Que c'est.

Less than lovers

More than friends

You are so fucking beautiful.

You are so fucking valid.

You are so fucking important.

You are so fucking intelligent.

You are so fucking cared about and loved.

How sweet it was

To be loved by you.

I wish it didn't leave this uncomfortable

aftertaste.

The crunch of cartilage

Cries of the guilty

Love for the loveless

Blood

So much blood

And snot

And begging

It was a monster who did not show mercy

It was a monster that wanted him to pay for
what they'd done

A monster that has to live with this

Their hair's a mess

Eyes are insane

Knuckles bloodied and bruised

It was devoid of the sunlight

The streetlamp shed itself onto violence and
wrath

Sexless Choking

Angered tears and a pleading cry

The blood shall never dry

Where is he now?

That wrathful monster,

The person turned demon for just a while

That scarred and smoking child?

Spitting blood

Helpless eyes

Pinned

Beaten

Defeated

Punished.

Her gratitude

A golden lining

The darling monster

A sacrifice for greater good

How it must have felt

To be forcibly fucked

Raw

Overpowered

She cried and begged for someone

To do something

Anything

Please

It was I who overheard

I who acted

I who shall carry the weight of hellish

violence

Ever and ever after.

It is your eyes, so beautiful and bright,

That remind me of the moon's wondrous light.

There are ghost and fiends that circle my head.

I sometimes wish I was dead,

But

I love the moon.

Hopefully,

I shall, soon,

Lay in your arms,

Safe, sound, from harm.

Bloodshot eyes

Unwashed hair

Cracked lips

Torn flesh

I am not romantic

Not beautiful

Not an angel.

Unintelligible

Metaphor

Commonplace

It is in your skin that I find solace

I place your value

In my tears

Your little waves and perfect imperfections
are part of you, and you are a thing of beauty.

There's someone better

I'm sorry

It's not me

I wish that I could die and be

One step closer to you

We fell asleep together

One last time

Closed our eyes

Pretended that we were still in love

That all was well outside

That the rain was something we invited.

Klimt and Satie whisked us away,

And life was anything but real.

Your skin was so soft, pleasant, quieting.

The face in the window and the man in the

ceiling went on vacation,

To give us a moment of clarity before their

inevitable return with the winds.

We hurt the ones we love,

And I loved you too much, it seemed.

It will come again, dearest.

We spend most of our time waiting on the feelings to return, and when we do, we never appreciate them when they should be appreciated.

With an unfathomable number of potential
partners,
Comes an equal amount of opportunity.

If only it were possible to know,

During the best times of my life,

How much I would miss them now.

Dried lilacs and summer snow

Weeping trees and creek's flow

Old memories hazed in a guise of flowers

Branches long since cut down

Fearsome butterflies and a frog with a crown

A young, battered man covered by lush life

somehow still, dreams of death.

Although she's always there, beside you

It's impossible not to feel alone,

As the sun has long since shone.

It's a metaphor, Hazel Grace;

Put the gun between your lips,

Splat your brains on the wall.

Surrounded by all those who love me

Yet I still feel alone.

They say she was born of the dirt,

A floral sapling.

Some thought it worth it to brave the thorns

In hopes that they may taste the berries she

bore only for a select few.

She twisted and sprawled and shed her leaves.

She gave fruit for the wrong person,

I hope she doesn't have to again.

She took root in maybe not the best of soil,

But still

She grows.

And grows.

They say she was born of the dirt,

Earthen and weathered.

She surely may grow taller than even the

biggest trees.

Nature is wrathful, and as such,

So is she.

I've found nothing to be more fleeting than

feeling.

We quickly grow uninterested,

It doesn't take too long to want something

else, or something more.

We quickly wish that things could be
different,
It doesn't take too long to think that the things
could be better.
We quickly change our tune,
It doesn't take too long for a song to get old.
We quickly leave each other's lives,
It doesn't take too long for the beautiful
person on the other side of the bed to be
replaced with someone else.
I've found no feeling more fleeting than
romance,
It dies just as it is born,
In a short moment.

First kiss with a boy

Don't tell anyone

It's not gay;

It's practice

Don't look at me from down there

And stop talking

You can't tell anyone

Please

No

No

No

Please

It hurts

Stop talking

Just let me finish

I didn't cry then, but I do now, six years later.
I'm sorry. I told some people recently. It got
too hard to keep to myself. No one knows your
name.

If only you could see your own body as I do.

You are a man, through and through.

There is none more handsome than you.

Your eyes are the kindest, your kisses divine.

To enjoy you, I needn't even bring wine.

I wish to gaze upon your beautiful masculine body forevermore,

And tell you how much I think of you.

I wish I wasn't afraid of being me.

Divided by things like *he* and *she,*

I very much do not want to be me.

It would be nice if things were simple,

Blank and white,

Unlike things that could be wrong or right.

Hello, Dearest, it's me. These days without you have been difficult, but I have managed to survive six days at least. It's become easier to understand, and I truly, truly do not blame you for the immense canyon I feel in my stomach. I could explain the logistics of it all, and describe to you my understanding of *why,* but I feel it is unnecessary as I am positive that you have done much in the way of thinking recently, just as I have. I desire, primarily, to thank you for everything you've been to me, during the hardest part of my life so far, and although you aren't here during my most recent loss (id est you), you have been instrumental in my being alive to write this for you now. I will be okay without you, I just would rather not be. All of the things that you unconditionally did for me, such as giving me a bath when I was covered in red/orange queso vomit, listening to me talk for hours about things that which bothered me, the company while watching *films* or the Office, being the body and mind that supported me both in physical and in emotional endeavors, and being so far my favourite cuddling and the sleeping companion (I think by now you get the point), are all things that are irreplaceable, unforgettable, and immeasurable in their value to me.

It has been a year since then. It is surreal how things change in such a short amount of time. The sentiment that you are irreplaceable, unforgettable, and immeasurable in value stands to this day. I would like to connect again, sometime. Thanks, Ash.

I had a babysitter once. I will not divulge their name or any other identifying information. This was many years ago, and I think they were underage as well, under 20, at least, but still much older than I was. I would have been about 6 or 7. My mom left the house and left me and presumably my younger brother under the care of a babysitter.

I remember the day well. It was cloudy, SpongeBob was on during the morning (R.I.P. Stephen Hillenburg, thank you for your art.), and we were playing with monster trucks my then father bought for us.

I had built a fort underneath the frame of a car-shaped bed I had. The frame extended above the mattress, and it was easy to drape a blanket over top of it, making a nice, secret base for my brother and I.

My brother was sleeping, and I was playing in the car bed fort. I had a stuffed penguin that Punky gave to me, and I think I may have been looking at my Pokémon cards.

It was dark under the blanket. The shades were drawn, it was late afternoon in the brisk Fort St John winter, I could barely see whatever it was I was doing. Dark like our stars and like our eyes.

The babysitter came into the fort. They had found one of my mother's vibrators. It was blue, with a dolphin-shaped clitoral stimulator coming from the main shaft of the vibrator. It had a white, studded base, and ran on a few AA batteries.

The babysitter took off her panties. I think they were purple, or pink, something to that effect. She licked the tip of the vibrator's main shaft, and in it went. She told me to watch. I didn't know what to do. I wasn't comfortable, but I didn't really know why. I sat there and watched as the blue toy whirred, and she moaned and giggled at me, making sure I was watching closely. She reached over and stroked my half-erect penis. I can't imagine there was much to stroke - I was quite young.

She left the vibrator in, holding it with one of her hands, and she bent over, resting her knees on either side of my legs.

She pulled down my white underwear, and she began to suck me off. I hated every moment of it. It felt gross. It felt wet and hot and just unsanitary. I didn't say anything. I started to cry, but I tried my best to stay quiet and wait for it to be over.

Her legs shook, she made a yelping noise, and it was over. I realize now that she must have came, and all I was to her was a vulnerable means to an end. I didn't start to talk about this incident until very recently. I just sort of knew it was one of those things that I shouldn't tell anyone about, like when someone would let me stay up late, or have a sip of their beer.

Here I am. Writing about abuse that took place about 12 or so years ago in hope that someone who is in the position I was in might gain the willpower to speak up.

There is strength in telling someone about your abuse. There is power and liberation that comes with accepting and identifying traumatic events in your life. If anyone reading this is currently experiencing some form of abuse, please, please do not stay quiet any longer than you must. I waited too long, as have many before us. Don't be another statistic.

I only think about you in the nighttime, only in
the nighttime
Endlessly, endlessly, your words are all I hear
in the silence that penetrates my walls.

Alongside all my puny sorrows, you swim through my memory, and sometimes, you pierce my heart.

Although it pains me so,

I wouldn't trade your thorny love for anything.

Thank you, pretty lady.

Of my many *what ifs*, you were my favourite.

A deaf songbird sings when it knows it is heard, not because it can sing well, but because its voice carries its love and its passion. A deaf songbird knows not how to whistle, but it sure can hum, and it sure tries its best to carry a tune. How romantic it feels to sing to your mate, doing your best, although you probably sound more like a cat than like a songbird.

A deaf songbird sings anyway.

Made in the USA
Columbia, SC
24 February 2020